Loves Me Not:
Healing and
Heartbreak God's Way

RENEE FISHER

Unless otherwise identified, all Scripture quotations in this publication are taken from the *Holy Bible, New International Version*® (NIV®). Copyright © 1973, 1978, 1984, 2011 by Biblica, Inc.® Used by permission of Zondervan. All rights reserved.

Cover © Dollar Photo Club
Cover Design by Hannah Rose Beasley
Back cover author photo © Kati Maxwell Photography

Copyright © 2015 Renee Fisher
http://www.ReneeFisher.com

ISBN: 1523617497
ISBN-13: 978-1523617494

LOVES ME NOT

DEDICATION

To anyone who has experienced the gut-wrenching
pain of a broken heart.

TABLE OF CONTENTS

INTRODUCTION: MY DREAM DIED

A t some point, you have to go all in.[1] Christians love to talk about "guarding your heart," especially in the context of relationships. There are countless how-to articles and dating books featuring chapter titles like "Ten Steps to Guard Your Heart and Your Significant Other's" or "How to Guard Your Heart Against a Breakup." But to me, it sounds like a cliché. And I hate clichés.

When it comes to our relationships, I think we're missing something. Jesus summarizes our highest command as:

> *"Love the Lord your God with all your heart and with all your soul and with all your mind and with all your strength.' The second is this: 'Love your neighbor as yourself.' There is no commandment greater than these" (Mark 12:30–31, NIV).*

If the heart is only one quarter of the greatest commandment in the Bible, why are we emphasizing the heart like it's the only factor in love?

And what of Jeremiah's claim that:

"The heart is deceitful above all things and beyond cure. Who can understand it?" (Jeremiah 17:9).

Perhaps love doesn't begin with romance—and goes much deeper than the heart.

GOING *ALL IN* FOR LOVE

According to Mark 12:30, Jesus wants us to be all in. And when we love Him with our all, it will help shape our perspective of earthly relationships, romantic and otherwise. When we are totally firm and secure in God's love for us, we will be less worried about *guarding our hearts* from pain and heartbreak as we relate to others.

Jesus is the greatest example of this. He loved His Father so much that He was not afraid of getting hurt by loving others. On the contrary, He died for relationships. Jesus sacrificed everything for love. He did this to restore not only our relationship with Him, but our relationships with each other. His body—not just His heart—was broken for us. Clearly, Jesus wasn't afraid of a broken heart, mind, or body. What would happen if we had the same perspective?

Relationships are risky business, and there's no guarantee you won't end up with a broken heart. But because of Christ's love, the fear of a broken heart no longer has to be the motivating factor.

1 John 4:18 (NIV) says, "There is no fear in love. But perfect love drives out fear, because fear has to do with punishment. The one who fears is not made perfect in love."

We can fulfill the greatest commandment because of God's perfect example in the flesh. Christ's mission was to leave paradise and sacrifice Himself on the altar of love. Even when it appears that Jesus struggles with going through with this plan, He prays:

"My Father, if it is not possible for this cup to be taken away unless I drink it, may your will be done" (Matthew 26:42).

His whole life was dedicated to making us whole; He loved us with His mind, body, heart, and strength, so that we might also be able to love wholly.

THE HEART'S BEST DEFENSE

In my early twenties, I was always afraid of getting into a relationship for fear I'd get hurt. I'd try to do everything perfectly. I tried the ten-inch rule (keeping ten inches between myself and a romantic interest at all times). I even joined a church group just to get to know a guy a little better in that context first.

Not that my behavior was wrong, but sometimes we can be more concerned with getting things right, and checking off all the relationship boxes, that we even miss the compatibility factor. The idea of being "in a relationship" just seems more appealing than being single. It's easy to obsess so much about getting relationships perfect that we forget about our most important relationship—our relationship with God.

When our concern for God becomes clouded or replaced entirely by pursuing, pleasing, and protecting our earthly relationships, we're in danger. If we're not paying attention, we can easily miss what God is trying to show us about our relationships.

Desire for (or fear of) finding a spouse isn't as important as our relationship with Him. He's ready to show us how much we can accomplish for Him, regardless of our relationship status.

From the moment we wake up to the moment we lay our heads down, we have the grand opportunity and honor to shower God with our love.

How can we love God with our all? Through prayer, thank God daily for the things He has so graciously given. Expectantly read the Word, asking God to speak. For the nature lovers, take a walk outdoors and remind yourself of God's creation and of your part in an incredible love story. For the person on the go, if your schedule won't allow any extra time, recall a verse from memory, or be mindful as you thank God for your meals. Over time, watch as your love grows while you remain in Him.

Spiritual discipline may not seem like the most glamorous relationship advice, but it can literally restore your heart, mind, body, and strength. The next time someone tells you the *just guard your heart* cliché, you can confidently share with him or her that the best defense of the heart is to first give it fully to God.

PART I: THE ANATOMY OF A RELATIONSHIP

CHAPTER 1: CHRISTIAN FRIENDSHIP

"Christian friendship is not simply about going to concerts together or enjoying the same sporting event. It is the deep oneness that develops as two people journey together toward the same destination, helping one another through the dangers and challenges along the way"
(Timothy Keller).[2]

I'd like to say I have friendship with the opposite sex figured out, and that I had a zillion male friends before my husband, but I didn't. Before I married Marc, it had been over eight years since my last serious relationship, which in my opinion does not count. And to be honest, I had a tough time being just friends with boys. I was the one who always wanted more.

I'm not the girl with the most dating experience either. I certainly hope you won't count my lack of guy friends against me, because one thing I do know now is what a healthy relationship looks like.

Now that I'm married I get it. If it weren't for my husband, Marc, I wouldn't be able to look back on my failed relationships, including those who were "just friends," to see what went wrong.

It is my hope to inspire and encourage you through your heartbreak to find healing God's way. As I open the storybook of my past, I want you to know there is such a thing as healthy friendship with the opposite sex!

WHAT IS TRUE FRIENDSHIP?

A true friend, as Timothy Keller writes, is a deep relationship between two people. What does that have to do with this book on breaking up?

A lot in fact.

Most relationships start off as friends and unfortunately (or fortunately) end up as friends. I don't know about you, but I hate *the friend zone*. It's pretty much the worst kind of relationship to get stuck or end up in. With today's hook-up-or-go-home culture, friendship with the opposite sex seems nearly impossible—especially before dating.

"Who needs another friend when you can just have sex?" says the world.

The church doesn't offer much help either. There are many Christian men who are afraid to pull the trigger when it comes to pursuing women, meanwhile there are also as many desperate women who assume if a guy asks her out that it means marriage. Yikes.

Since when did men and women fear a coffee date? Do we need another reason to support the fact that breakups hurt?

Don't answer that!

CAN WE JUST BE FRIENDS?

Ii is possible for guys and girls to be just friends. It's best to start with questions like:

What is the best way to become friends with the opposite sex when I'm quite busy with work, come from a small town, or don't go to church with a singles group?
What's an appropriate amount of time to be friends before making the next step, and who should make it and when?

Questions like these are very important to ask before marriage, *but* before I attempt to answer these questions, I want to start with friendship.

Godly friendship, regardless of sex, looks a lot different from the world. Let's take a look at what the Word says about the definition of friendship.

- Friends don't gossip about each other (Proverbs 26:20).
- Friends are gentle instead of harsh or angry at each other (Proverbs 15:1).
- Friends words bring healing (Proverbs 12:18).
- Friends should be quick to listen, slow to speak, and slow to become angry (James 1:19).
- Friends don't destroy each other (Proverbs 11:9).
- Friends are understanding and even-tempered with each other (Proverbs 17:2).
- Friends pray for each other (Job 42:10, James 5:16).
- Friends spur each other forward (Hebrews 10:24).
- Friends encourage each other daily (see Hebrews 3:13).
- Friends share in each other's troubles and joys (see Romans 12:15).
- Friends are reliable and stick closer than a brother or sister (Proverbs 18:24).

In other words, Christian friends are honest, open, and transparent with one another (or H.O.T.), as a pastor friend of mine Tim Ross says. You may not want to confess just anything or everything to the opposite sex—or right away. A great question to ask:

Do you have any friendships with the opposite sex whom you aren't able to be honest with? Why or why not?

There is a fine line between judging someone's sin and bringing up a concern about a friend to his or her attention.

Be compassionate. Use a helpful tone so the other person doesn't doubt your sincerity. Also, make sure to check yourself and remove your own hypocrisy before making your friend aware of his or her faults (see Matthew 7:3).

We all have blind spots. No one should be at fault for being unaware, but once you know, then it becomes your responsibility to do something about it. Think of at least one friend you can be bold with. Take time to schedule a coffee date or lunch, and ask them when life gets busy to check in and see how you're doing.

Everybody needs an accountability partner or someone who doesn't take the excuse "I'm busy" to make sure you're doing okay! Your friend should make you want to act like a better person.

Everybody has bad days, but your friend or romantic interest should leave you more encouraged than drained.

What's one nice thing you can do for your friend to let him or her know that you care? What's one nice thing you wish someone would do for you?

Take inventory of your relationships and find out if this could be what's leading to disappointment, and then don't be afraid to talk about it with the other person.

Text messages, e-mails, and Facebook or Twitter messages leave plenty of room for misinterpretation. The best way to reconcile a relationship is face-to-face with that person. Instead of gossiping or spreading rumors, take the time to clear things up first before going to other people. Expectations can lead to disappointment.

Maybe you're expectations are too high or too low.

If you find your friends to be one-sided, ask yourself the questions below to determine why your friends aren't as quick to bear your burdens as you are theirs.

Best friends support each other in good times and bad. They desire only the best for the other person. Sometimes we are afraid to take inventory of our friendships for fear we'll discover that some are only there when times are good.

Do you find it's easier to be there for someone else than for you? Why do you think this is so?

Oftentimes, the way you appreciate others being there for you doesn't equal what others need from you.

Friendship is a two-way street. Maybe try setting a few healthy boundaries first, and then ask yourself if there is anyone in your life who tends to lean more on the dramatic side of life—meaning he or she is always in need of comfort, encouragement, and support.

There are plenty of ways to be a great friend through your time, talents, and resources, including money and referrals. Maybe you can't personally meet his or her needs, but you can always help assist in getting their needs met.

RENEE FISHER

Do you know of a friend in need whom you could refer to another friend, mentor, or someone you trust for help?

No friend is identical. God created each one unique—this is what makes friendship so special. After reading the list on page twelve, I hope you know and understand more about what a true friend does and doesn't look like.

There was nowhere in the definition of a friend list that said you can or can't be friends with the opposite sex. Nowhere does the Bible say, "Thou shall or shall not be friends with the opposite sex."

Praise God, right?

But it does say to choose your friends "carefully" (Proverbs 12:26, NIV).

Maybe after reading the list you'll know more about your motives and the intentions of the friends surrounding you. It is also my hope to instill a deeper sense of appreciation for what it takes to be friends first before jumping into a relationship. What better way to discern if a relationship will be a good fit if you know what good of a friend he or she is first.

I do believe it is possible for guys and girls to be just friends. The how is between you, God, and the other person.

Let's look at the heart of the matter in the next chapter, shall we?

CHAPTER 2: THE HEART OF THE MATTER

*"We need not be ashamed that our hearts ache; that
we need and thirst and hunger for much more. All of
our hearts ache. All of our hearts are at some level
unsatisfied and longing. It is our insatiable need for
more that drives us to…God"*
(John & Stasi Eldredge)[3]

The Merriam-Webster Dictionary defines heartbreak as a *crushing grief, anguish, or distress.*[4] I know I've been there *many times.* Maybe you've been there not once, but many times as well. I want to share with you this one time when dating made me throw up in my mouth a little.

Sounds extreme, but then again, so am I. I was struggling with my anxiety. I was struggling with being single. I was struggling with my job. I was struggling with trust issues.

In the middle of my heartbreak, a guy friend showed up at my apartment with hugs and to surprise me with my favorite cheesecake. He knew I needed a friend.

We sat next to each other on the couch, but we didn't kiss. We watched a movie, but he left after I ate my cheesecake. I couldn't understand how a guy could be so caring and thoughtful. Sure, I had plenty of people to talk to, but it almost felt better in the arms of a stranger.

He hugged me.

He listened.

He was kind.

Suddenly, I was woken up violently in the middle of the night to puke my guts out through the morning.

It was awful, and it felt like the flu. Because my life was such a mess, it took me a while to realize my heartbreak—*not* the flu—made me throw up in my mouth a little. It was so embarrassing to admit to my roommate, my parents, and those closest to me that I struggled with panic attacks so severe that I couldn't help but throw up, especially when it came to matters of the opposite sex.

It was also embarrassing to admit to my guy friend that I couldn't date him back. I wanted so desperately to be loved, romanced, and in a relationship with someone who was caring, but I wasn't *ready* to date.

It wasn't enough to *know* I wasn't ready— my body forced me to stop dating.

My heart felt locked up in prison. I hated the thought that I, at the age of twenty-six, needed to set boundaries in dating to figure out my messy life. But I did.

I dug deep in the Scriptures.

I sought counseling again.

I got back on anxiety medication.

I quit my job.

I started my writing career.

I wish I could tell you that I gave myself grace for feeling like a failure. To give myself the same grace my guy friend was trying to give me, but was so violently afraid to receive. The same grace God already gave me while dying a violent death on the cross for my sins. I'd also like to say that everything got better instantly. Or that I had some radical transformation. I didn't.

It was a step-by-step, day-by-day process to learn how to love myself, accept myself, and forgive myself for my many flaws.

God knew I needed the journey. He knew how much I needed to be broken so I could learn how to sing His praises again, and He knew when to bring the right guy into my life. The kind of guy that made me feel safe till "death do us part."

YOU HAVE TO KISS A LOT OF FROGS

There's a popular phrase that says you have to kiss a lot of frogs before you find a prince.

But what happens if it's one frog too many?

The one where I said *no,* and he didn't stop. On a cold, dark day in February, 2006, *it* happened. A new coworker asked me to drinks after work. He seemed harmless enough, and I honestly didn't think twice about saying yes. We drove to a nearby brewery and each ordered one drink.

One drink too many.

One drink for a supposedly "friendly" coworker to turn aggressive.

I don't know why I agreed to take one car. My car. After drinks he asked me to go to the beach. I reluctantly said yes because it was cold, and because I thought he said dinner would follow.

After we sat on the sand for a while, he kissed me. I felt uncomfortable, but because we took my car, I didn't know what else to do. I persuaded him to go back to the car. I wanted food. He wanted me to park. Since we couldn't decide where to go to next, I parked.

That was a BIG mistake.

That's when it happened.

I said *no*, but he kept going. I tried saying *no* once. I said *no* twice. Finally, I panicked and said *NOOOOOO* for the third time. But it was already too late. I saw things I never wanted to see until my wedding night.

There are no words to describe the shame and humiliation that followed that ride back to his car. I drove as fast as I could and forced him out. He tried being nice all of a sudden, but I didn't want to hear any apologies. I was done trying to be the nice girl.

He took something from me that would take me years to get back—my dignity. I burst into tears and sobbed more than I ever had in my entire life. Looking back, I can't believe I made it home while driving and sobbing with fogged over windows. On my way home, I dialed my boss's number and left her a voice mail to explain the situation. I certainly wasn't expecting to get in trouble for reaching out to my boss for help.

Because the "incident" happened after hours, I was on my own. I shouldn't have called her that night. There was nothing my company could do to help me. Of course he lied to both my boss and his. He told all sorts of things to get out of trouble.

Somehow this mess became entirely my fault because I was the one who agreed to a drink after work.

This guy knew I was a virgin.

He also knew he could take advantage of me and continued harassing me at work.

Of course he would be the *only* person I could see from my desk. Every day he would slam the door and curse at me in Spanish under his breath—anything to make me feel miserable.

When I finally had the courage to confront him at work, he told me to stop acting like a fourteen-year-old girl. In other words, he was mad because I didn't give him what he wanted that night in my car.

Seriously gross.

I felt used and helpless.

I finally caught him at work with an inappropriate e-mail, but then he suddenly changed his story.

The same guy who told me he had an ex-wife said he was now *married* and that I was the one who was falsely trying to get him fired. All lies. I felt so naive. I started having panic attacks again, and I didn't know what to do next. My parents didn't know how to help me. HR told me if I brought up the issue again I'd get written up.

I was the one who said no, so how was it my fault?

I wrote these words on my blog a few days later from Streams in the Desert, my favorite devotional, because I had no one else to turn to:

"Do not take revenge, my friends" (Romans 12:19, NIV).

"There are times when doing nothing demands much greater strength than taking action. Maintaining composure is often the best evidence of power. Even to the vilest and deadliest of charges. Jesus responded with deep, unbroken silence. His silence was so profound that it caused His accusers and spectators to wonder in awe.

Men may misjudge your aim, Think they have cause to blame, Say, you are wrong; Keep on your quiet way, Christ is the Judge, not they, Fear not, be strong."[5]

The apostle Paul said, "None of these things move me" (Acts 20:24, KJV). He did not say, "None of these things *hurt* me."

NOT MY FAULT

Looking back, I know now it wasn't my fault. Even though I said yes to drinks, that didn't mean an open invitation to take advantage of me. Clearly!

There are men in this world—bad men—who take advantage of women. Like the man who shot his girlfriend in the face in front of their three-month-old baby girl and then shot himself. Like the young man who killed his mother and then drove to her school and killed 20 helpless children and six adults.

Maybe there's nothing you or I can do in the moment but feel helpless in heartbreak, but I do know there is God who sees me—sees us.

And one day He's coming back again to judge the earth and redeem His people. Until then, I keep pressing on.

YOUR WHOLE HEART

Heartbreak cripples. It's caused me to lose my cheesecake once. And another time it took advantage of me—even when I said *no*. I've also been sidelined by panic attacks, and as I just shared, I kissed *one too many* frogs. It's amazing that my heart is whole (healed).

The most frustrating part in sharing both of those stories was revisiting the fear I felt at that time. If only I could reach out to my former self and tell her that one day very soon she will meet her prince.

But isn't that what faith is all about?

*"Our hearts are enlarged by Jesus. And by that, we mean that we must be willing to be honest with him and with ourselves about the true nature of our souls—our sorrows, our desires, our dreams, our fears, our deepest and scariest hopes."*⁶

You never know when an incident—whether bad or good—is going to happen to change the entire course of your life. That's why it's important to stay in the Word and in prayer, so that you are able to stand firm against heartbreak when the trials come (Ephesians 6:13).

Here is a list of twenty-seven types I've complied by doing a "heart" search in the Bible to find healing for your broken heart. Feel free to write down your favorite verses, or make up your own list.

- Do you have a praying heart? (Genesis 24:45)
- Do you have a hardened heart? (Exodus 7:3, 9:35)
- Do you have a fiery heart? (Deuteronomy 5:4, 24)
- Do you have a judgmental heart? (1 Samuel 16:7)
- Do you have a wise and understanding heart? (1 Kings 3:12, Proverbs 2:10)
- Do you have a whole heart? (1 Chronicles 28:9, 29:17)
- Do you have a faithful and undivided heart? (2 Chronicles 15:17, 16:9b)
- Do you have a faint heart? (Job 23:16)
- Do you have a lustful heart? (Job 31:7, Matthew 5:28)
- Do you have an examined heart? (Psalm 17:3)
- Do you have a pure heart? (Psalm 24:4, 2 Timothy 2:22)
- Do you have a sad heart? (Psalm 42:5, 42:11, 43:5)
- Do you have a broken and repentant heart? (Psalm 51:17)
- Do you have a hidden heart? (Psalm 119:11)

- Do you have a guarded heart? (Proverbs 4:23, Philippians 4:7)
- Do you have a happy or heavy heart? (Proverbs 14:13, 30; 15:13)
- Do you have a captured heart? (Song of Solomon 4:9)
- Do you have a deceitful heart? (Jeremiah 17:9)
- Do you have a single heart? (Ezekiel 11:19)
- Do you have a new heart? (Ezekiel 36:26)
- Do you have a torn heart? (Joel 2:13)
- Do you have a treasured heart? (Matthew 6:21)
- Do you have a good or evil heart? (Matthew 12:35)
- Do you have an anxious heart? (Luke 21:34)
- Do you have a taken heart? (John 16:33)
- Do you have a holy heart? (2 Corinthians 1:22)
- Do you have a thankful heart? (Colossians 3:16, 4:2)

After reading through this list, I hope you have a better understanding of what it looks like to have a whole heart—one that rests safely in the arms of Jesus.

There should be no more doubts that a healed heart can happen. It is possible!

Maybe it takes time.

Maybe it takes lots of time.

The healing process is different for each person, and each relationship is different as well.

In the next chapter, we'll learn how to handle a relationship that has become an idol and what to do about it.

PART II: BREAKING UP IS HARD TO DO

CHAPTER 3: BREAKING UP WITH IDOLS

"You shall not make for yourself an image in the form of anything in heaven above or on the earth beneath or in the waters below"
(Exodus 20:4).

I do not want to get into another relationship unless God's in it. No more regrets.

Have you ever had to break up with someone because he or she consumed your entire life to the point where God was no longer the center?

I have.

You're not alone

I remember writing in my journal after a breakup that I needed to *leave room for the cravings of God.* That's what my heart longed for. It wasn't really about the relationship anymore. It was more about the fighting, and who was *right* or *wrong.*

He said.

She said.

Our plans had all melted into something that resembled an idol. We worshipped our relationship because we were more scared of the breakup—and being single.

I am the best friend you will ever have.

I'm the one.

You're my soul mate.

Hearing words like that from someone who couldn't commit almost ripped my world apart. I don't know about you, but that is not the kind of relationship I want. I'm never, ever going back to that again (thanks Taylor Swift for releasing that song too many years too late). Faith is what you and I need after heartbreak.

"Now faith is confidence in what we hope for and assurance about what we do not see" (Hebrews 11:1, NIV).

It's hard to remain single—especially if you're not a very patient person. You must wait on God. He must be your one and only. Breaking up with idols is necessary.

"You shall not make for yourself an image in the form of anything in heaven above or on the earth beneath or in the waters below" (Exodus 20:4, NIV).

NO REGRETS

I have a hard time letting go of the past. I used to ask questions like,

"How can I move on when my ex said we were going to get married? When he told me he loved me and wanted to spend the rest of my life with him?"

For the longest time any thought or mention of my ex, Jake (not his real name), would send me reeling. I regretted everything I ever said or did.

I even regretted loving him.

It took me a few years to realize the error of my thinking. Neither you nor I can control the outcome of any relationship. There is no fear in love (1 John 4:18).

We can choose whom to love, and by God's grace we are loved in return—even though a relationship may end.

Maybe it's like that with you and your ex. Maybe you regret every single thing about the relationship. I have a couple questions for you:

How would you grow? What would you learn?

Every relationship is worth learning from—even the bad ones. I didn't want to break up with my ex because he was the only person I assumed I would spend the rest of my life with. Jake was my idol. He said he was the only one for me, which is why the breakup was so hard. I genuinely thought I loved him and cared for him.

I wish I could say the same about other, lesser breakups. The ones who said they were the best I would ever have and then continued to make my life miserable at the thought of leaving. You know what that is called? Manipulation. Even though I couldn't say that back then, I can now and without fear. I needed to learn how to smash the idol of relationships and squelch the fears before I let myself really get hurt.

A broken heart is the worst. Don't you agree?

Before I met my husband, my last serious relationship taught me an important lesson that I'll never forget. Breaking up with someone isn't just about religion (God told me).

It's also not just an emotional high. I had to make the choice to worship God and no one else.

Not a boyfriend.
Not a bank account.
Not even a new pair of shoes (ouch).

STOP TRYING TO CHANGE HIM

There is a verse in the Bible that says to weep with those who weep and rejoice with those who rejoice (Romans 12:15).

Here's another that says,

"Praise be to the God and Father of our Lord Jesus Christ, the Father of compassion and the God of all comfort, who comforts us in all our troubles, so that we can comfort those in any trouble with the comfort we ourselves received from God" (2 Corinthians 1:3–4, NIV).

It doesn't say anywhere in the Bible not to comfort others with heartbreak. It also doesn't say you must try and change the person in his or her heartbreak. That's where I stumble and fall so many times.

When I look back on my past relationships, I feel like I am the person to blame because I tried to change the other person in the relationship.

Including relationships with the same sex. I wanted the best for my friend (guy or girl) even if they couldn't see it at the time.

When I didn't get the results I desired, I became more forceful. This is where I find the thin line between wanting and doing what's best for others.

They have to want it too.

I'm just going to pause right there and let the last sentence sink in. If you're anything like me, it feels a little bit like a punch to the gut or a heart check. I need help with that one.

"Hi, my name is Renee, and I have a control problem." It's scary how badly I tried to get the other person to change even at the expense of our relationship.

Dietrich Bonhoeffer, one of my favorite theologians and a martyr of the Christian faith, said:

"He who loves his dream of a [guy or girl] more than the Christian itself becomes a destroyer of the latter, even though his personal intentions may be ever so honest and earnest and sacrificial…Our ideals should never be realized at any cost. They are not worth having if they destroy others in the process of their actualization."[7]

If I didn't push too hard, maybe our relationship didn't have to end. Maybe that's why I had regrets.

MEET MORGAN

I want you to meet my friend Morgan MacGavin. She lives in Nashville, TN, and is currently attending *Liberty University Online*. We know each other through mutual friends, and although we have never met in person, we've talked on the phone numerous times and prayed with each other. I hope her breakup story inspires you to know you're not the only one who has trouble letting go of an ex.

"If I place all the years prior to twenty aside, I'm left with a decade worth of moments that, when you dissect them, all come down to one thing: *love*.

My heart absolutely aches when I look back at that girl, knowing how empty she felt inside, and for how long. Drinking and cutting were only temporary fixes.

I found myself justifying sleeping with one man while dating another simply because neither one made me feel whole, but together, bits and pieces of me felt filled in. Then "he" came along.

I'll never forget the first time I told him "I love you." The words "I'm not sure you want to say that" should always be a ginormous red flag.

A few months later, he met my older brother.

To put it mildly, it didn't go well. That night is when my boyfriend chose to say the three words I'd been longing to hear. His timing was impeccable. The events of that day would be what ultimately led to me to end my relationships with most of my family.

I didn't need any of them or their thoughts on how controlling he was, or how I wasn't the real me with him.

We often discussed marriage, but whenever I brought up having kids, he would reply that he already had one. He had a daughter, and while being a mom was far from anything I wanted or was ready for at the time, I knew that's what *he* wanted.

He was thinking of being a Buddhist, so God was out. The girl he told everything to was not me. He defended his *friend* when I got upset over a link to porn she'd posted on his Facebook. I felt bad for making him feel guilty over the pictures of other girls I'd discovered on his laptop.

I loved him so much.

It was a Saturday night when he called. I heard the words "I haven't loved you in a while" and "I don't see a future with us." Lying in a tight ball in my bed, I wailed from the pain.

The silence around me was so loud. I had no one, not even myself, because that girl was somewhere on the other end of a disconnected phone line.

In my twenties I learned to stockpile pills. You never knew when you might need a high, or need to sell them. Every day for two weeks I rolled the prescription bottle around in my hand, taking just enough to keep me numb. I screamed at God every chance I could. This was just one more thing in a long list from my life.

I didn't want to be here anymore.

Two weeks later, with words that were not my own, I asked a friend,

"Can I go to church with you tomorrow?"

The next morning, I listened as the pastor spoke about shattered dreams. He said,

"What do you do when life doesn't turn out the way you thought it would turn out? What do you do when God doesn't show up the way you expected Him to?"

And then he read John 16:33 (NIV):

"I have told you these things, so that in me you may have peace. In this world you will have trouble. But take heart! I have overcome the world."

Almost instantly, a new ache filled my heart as tears fell down my face.

I wanted *that*.

I wanted love that brings peace.

It was like God spoke directly to me saying, "You can have that, Morgan. I never left you." Three months later, on July 18, 2010, I accepted Christ and was baptized.

Sometimes, surviving your twenties is as simple and as complex as a four-letter word most of us are either too scared to speak, or too scared not to. As humans we can spend a lifetime trying to put a square peg in a round hole. But if we stop focusing on our struggle just long enough, we have the beautiful opportunity to see that God has been holding out the right peg the entire time. We just have to choose to reach out and grab it.

NOT ALONE

In every book I write, I purposely add others input because I recognize my voice only counts as one. I very much hate being the only voice.

Honestly, it's your stories that help me to see that I'm not the only crazy person with a bad breakup story.

Below are real quotes from people like you. I hope you find their stories encouraging. You're not alone.

Jennifer, 33, said: "I try not to be, but I still have feelings of anger and ill will. Stupid *boy*."

Alicia, 29, said: "Taylor Swift and Kelly Clarkson helped me through the breakup. I'm married now with a gorgeous daughter. I never would have gotten there without him."

Amanda, 24, said: "I have moments, but for the most part I'm not bitter. I can tell based on my reactions to hearing things about my exes and/or seeing them around town. What helped me through the breakup was lots and lots of prayer. Daily Mass, Eucharistic adoration, spending time with friends who never judged me for feeling whatever it is I felt at the time."

D.D., 28, said: "I'm not bitter. Instead there is still guilt, and I still miss him. I wonder sometimes if I really did right."

Anonymous, said: "It's a tough call. I felt like the other person wanted to break up while I didn't. But he was not being honest and forthright, so in the end I did it. I wish the other person had been honest, even if it hurt my feelings, because the emotional turmoil was greater due to the dishonesty."

K, 27, said: "I feel like he made a mistake when he left me, and we should have worked it out. I think our relationship ended because there wasn't enough communication between us."

Crystal, 29, said: "I've never experienced a breakup."

Debra, 22, said: "No breakup history. Sorry to be so boring!"

Alice 33, said: "I don't care to run into my last ex ever again. I do pray for him and his family from time to time."

Jaimie, 36, said: "I don't have any regrets, but I wish I would have ended the relationship with my (former) best friend. I'm better, but I'm not bitter."

Monique, 37, said: "I trust too quickly."

Brenda, 36, said: "What helped me through the breakup was mainly time and rehashing it with friends over and over. Of course, now looking back, I wish I turned to God more and did more self-reflection. I want to prevent the same mistakes from happening again. I was not true to myself and who I was. I wanted to be married more than anything, and dated people I was not compatible with or who were not good for me. So it ended (by the grace of God) when it became impossible to wear the mask anymore. I became real. I shouldn't have dated them in the first place."

Alexandrea, 27, said: "My last relationship ended for so many reasons. I am okay but there are moments that I feel [regret] about it, because I feel like he should've been patient with me in understanding how frustrating it was for me. For the most part though, I realize that we both made mistakes in just not knowing how to deal with the situation. I can tell I am still bitter though sometimes—just because I still get disappointed in myself or angry with him for leaving."

Sheri, 24, said: "My then-boyfriend dumped me during the biggest trial of my life. I had been raped a month before and wasn't myself. For the first time in my life, I wasn't doing well. Anyway, when he dumped me, I felt like I had nothing. I had to face all of the pain that I was running from. This is when I got my relationship with God back on track. I didn't know where else to turn. Instead of crying myself to sleep, I would read my Bible, and it brought me such peace. That's when I realized I was bitter and needed the Holy Spirit to help me forgive."

Shari, 36, said: "It took me over a year to recover. He didn't want to be with someone who had had cancer and may be sick again. After a year, I *never* even remotely saw a selfish side to him until then. So very sad."

Krista, 28, said: "One of my breakups was due to his porn addiction. I can still remember the pain caused by several of my exes. At times I can still feel the pain, but no longer do I hate any of my exes. In fact, I think the biggest indication that I no longer have any regrets is that I can honestly say I wish them well, and I was happy to see when several of my exes got married and had kids."

Julianna, 24, said: "I was the breakup-er every time. Oh yeah, baby, I'm not proud of it. Some were going in different directions, others were jerk guys, and one just had no future. I'm happily married now, and though some of the guys I loved (with all my heart), I can see them as a little stepping stone toward the one God was preparing for me."

Arleen, 27, said: "My mom is a therapist and helped me when I hit rock bottom, which involved lots of crying and intense prayer on my bedroom floor. Thank God the relationship ended, because neither one of us were equipped to be a spouse, let alone for each other."

Kathleen, 30, said: "The relationship was toxic on so many levels. Mostly me abandoning all of the values I held dear. There was no actual partnership, nor was there trust. Many of our fights involved letting the other person know they would never be valued more than a certain level, or arguing about the level of intimacy with friends of the opposite sex."

Emily, 27, said: "I'm grateful for everything I've learned and the chances to know and celebrate my exes. They're all amazing men with great strengths, even if we're not together"

Kathy, 39, said: "I wish I had called the police any number of times when the abuse occurred. That will forever be the biggest regret of my life. I feel the leadership at my church failed me. I had a group of pals who held me up, listened, prayed, and came alongside me. I grew so much deeper because of the divorce. I really clung to God because friends have their own lives. My family was there, too, but they all live in other places."

Aren't you glad to know you're not the only one with (or without) a breakup story? I've said it once, and I'll say it again: you are not alone. Maybe this time I don't have to yell as loud.

If you remember nothing else from this book, remember that you're worth pursuing. I know it may be hard to read that just now, but it's true. I'll go into more of that in Part III, but for now, flip to the next chapter and let's dissect the proper ways of breaking up with someone.

CHAPTER 4: HOW TO BREAK UP WITH SOMEONE

"Do to others what you would have them do to you."
—*The Golden Rule*

I posted a question on Facebook recently, which asked,

"Is it ever appropriate to break up with someone over text, e-mail, phone, or social media?"

Let's be honest. You and I have committed at least one of these atrocities during our adolescent or adult lives. If not, I offer you a hearty congrats. Even if you weren't technically dating, it still hurts to be on the receiving end of one of those shrug-offs.

Maybe you stopped responding to his texts. Maybe you didn't return her phone calls. Maybe you hit the Delete button and proceeded to block incoming calls.

Don't get me started about social media.

I believe there are many books on the subject of dating and relationships because we (Christians) can't quite make up our minds.

One minute courting is "in," and the next minute dating is "in." You get the picture. In the last chapter I mentioned breaking up with idols, and how important it is not to place any man or woman before your relationship with God. This now leaves me with a couple very important questions:

Is there a right or wrong way to break up with someone? How do you know?

GOD TOLD ME TO BREAK UP WITH YOU

Would you agree Christians tend to over-spiritualize things, including breakups? One of the most common phrases used in Christian circles is "God told me to break up with you."

My friend Allison Fallon, writer and thinker and author of *Packing Light: Thoughts on Living Life with Less Baggage*, believes in becoming brave enough to live and tell the truth.

I asked her to share five reasons why you should *not* say,

"God told me to break up with you."

ALLISON'S STORY

There are a couple of things you learn when you grow up fully immersed in Christian culture. You learn how to rock out to DC Talk's "Jesus Freak," how to entertain yourself without a TV, how to sunbathe in a one-piece swimsuit, how to "date" in groups.

And how to blame God for your breakups.

It doesn't surprise me that this happens, by the way. I don't even think we're lying as the words slip out of our mouths:

"God told me to break up with you…"

I just think it's too tempting to pass the pain of the situation on to something or someone else. God seems like a good enough scapegoat, so we use Him.

Do I think it's impossible that God would prompt you to break up with someone?

Not at all. God cares about you and your circumstances, and He does sometimes whisper things that He wants us to know. Sometimes He does this audibly, but more often than not it happens in the deepest part of us, like a sudden knowing in our souls.

Either way, I think it sucks as a breakup line. Here's why:

God told me to break up with you hides the real reason for the breakup. If God wants you to break up with someone, there's a reason. He doesn't just walk around issuing random commands to His children without a purpose or plan.

So if you've felt a growing unrest, that sense that you do not want to be in this relationship anymore, don't ignore the feeling. Just ask yourself:

Why am I feeling this way?

Maybe you don't feel respected. Maybe you don't share the same values as your significant other. Maybe he or she did something you disagree with. Or maybe it's just really practical:

"I just don't see our lives fitting together long-term."

Regardless of the reason, it's important to communicate these reasons in the breakup. It helps you to define yourself and your boundaries, and it does the same thing for your girlfriend or boyfriend.

God told me to break up with you makes God the bad guy. If I were God, I'd be pretty frustrated that people kept blaming their crap on me. When a relationship goes south, we all share fault. Everyone involved. Well, all of us except for God. He didn't do it. He didn't make us get in the relationship, and He's not making us get out of it. So let's all stop blaming it on Him.

God told me to break up with you manipulates the situation. Rather than saying,

"I'm making this decision and I'm not going to change my mind," it's a really easy way to keep the doors of the relationship open.

It's like, "Yes, God told me to break up with you, but He didn't tell me if He was going to ask me to get back together with you anytime soon. I'll keep you posted when I hear from Him again."

This protects our fear of loneliness and rejection. It's also manipulative and wrong. Side note: It isn't manipulative to say,

"I need a break, and I'm not sure how long it will be. I don't expect you to wait while I figure out what I'm feeling, but I could be ready to talk again in a couple of weeks."

God told me to break up with you confuses the nature of God. I think too many of us think of God as a boss, rather than a dad. Donald Miller talks about this in his Storyline Conference, and it has really struck a chord with me. If we think of God as a boss, watching our every move, dictating orders to us down from above, we end up feeling really angry at Him, especially when life is hard.

"God made me do it," we tell ourselves, and distance ourselves from Him.

Our resentment builds. But God isn't like that. He guides us, advises us, coaxes us, and teaches us like a dad. He even disciplines us, but God doesn't boss us around.

He doesn't sit at the dinner table, dictating when we can eat our peas and when we can start on our chicken. He puts the food in front of us, and asks us to share a meal with Him.

God told me to break up with you ignores the control you have. The more we wake up to the control we have over our lives, the happier we'll be. The more ownership we take, the more we'll embrace the challenges we face, because they're not a punishment, they're just part of it.

They're the beauty and the magic of it. If we're busy blaming everything on God, we miss out on that.

HOW TO BREAK UP WITH SOMEONE

There are other examples of how we break up with someone. No matter if you're the one who broke up with him or her or the break-ee, it hurts. Maybe you're currently wondering how to end your relationship. Questions like:

"Is text, email, phone, or social media ever appropriate?"
"What kind of language should I use without sounding bitter?"
"How and when should I tell my friends? Social media? The whole world?"

In the history of breakups, many people have used, overused, and abused cliché phrases:

"I think we're better off as just friends."
"I'm just not that into you."
"It's not you, it's me."
"God told me to break up with you."
"You're not the one for me."
"I'm just not ready to date."

"I'm going to take a break from dating to date God."

"Our lives are just going in two separate directions."

The list could go on and on. I appreciate how one woman answered my breakup survey for this book. Tara answered and said,

"Truth is, I sold myself the lie for a false representation of love."

I can relate. I recently attended a women's Valentine's luncheon. We sat around the table eating and discussing what is love. One of the ladies read from 1 Corinthians 13 (read below).

"If I speak in the tongues of men and of angels, but have not love, I am only a resounding gong or a clanging cymbal. If I have the gift of prophecy and can fathom all mysteries and all knowledge, and if I have a faith that can move mountains, but have not love, I am nothing. If I give all I possess to the poor and surrender my body to the flames, but have not love, I gain nothing. Love is patient, love is kind. It does not envy, it does not boast, it is not proud. It is not rude, it is not self-seeking, it is not easily angered, it keeps no record of wrongs.

Love does not delight in evil but rejoices with the truth. It always protects, always trusts, always hopes, always perseveres. Love never fails…And now these three remain: faith, hope and love. But the greatest of these is love."

I've read 1 Corinthians 13 a thousand times, so I wasn't expecting anything new. It wasn't so much what love is, but what love *isn't*.

This is the thought that hit me square in the jaw: if you truly care about someone you were dating, courting, or whatever, you'll breakup with him or her *in love*. Even if you were never *in* love.

Get it?

Matthew 7:12, also known as the Golden Rule, says,

"So in everything, do to others what you would have them do to you" (NIV).

Ouch! I don't know about you, but when I'm hurt I usually do *not* respond in love. Nine times out of ten, my tone is nasty and so are my words. Please don't get me started on my body language.

I become completely closed off to love, at which point I am only looking out for myself and my own survival.

Isaiah 53:7 says, "He was oppressed and afflicted, yet he did not open his mouth" (NIV).

We can learn from Jesus who was falsely accused.

"Surely he took up our pain and bore our suffering, yet we considered him punished by God, stricken by him, and afflicted. But he was pierced for our transgressions, he was crushed for our iniquities; the punishment that brought us peace was on him, and by his wounds we are healed" (Isaiah 53:4–5).

Breaking up with someone may be the most difficult thing you've ever had to do. You may have a wounded heart, but because of Jesus' wounds you are *healed*. Before making your final decision, here are a few simple questions to think and pray through before ending the relationship.

Is your relationship hindering your relationship with God?

Consider taking a break for a few days or a week. Sometimes relationships get off track and need refocusing. This doesn't necessarily mean relationship death, but a simple time-out.

Is your relationship becoming more physical than you're comfortable with?

Everyone struggles with sexual temptation. If you have blood coursing through your veins, it's only natural to struggle with temptation.

However, it's when thoughts turn into actions that they become sin (1 Corinthians 10:13). Instead of skirting to find the line, talk to God and then your partner about proper boundaries.

Are you unsure of where your relationship stands?

The dreaded DTR (Define The Relationship) talk may be in order. Sometimes one person is more into the relationship than the other. Maybe he wants to get married, but she's freaking out. Maybe she needs to finish school, and he's just looking to have a good time.

Take time to pray and find God's purpose to establish a sure foundation, or maybe it's time to end the relationship.

After thinking long and hard, you may feel breaking up is the right thing to do. Ask God to give you strength in love. Maybe your boyfriend didn't treat you right, so a short conversation in a public place will do.

Maybe your girlfriend is prone to crying and would appreciate a more private setting to avoid embarrassment. Maybe your schedules won't allow for a face-to-face meeting right away. If you really care about someone, you'll wait to say your peace in person.

Sometimes the best way to find closure is not to end the relationship in anger or haste. It may cause you more pain. If you're like me, it's hard to wait to act when I know something must be done. This has been the theme of my life. During the times when I took control and sped up the process, I found myself in a bitter party of one.

No matter how much you feel he or she doesn't deserve to be broken up with in love, would you want to be broken up in that manner? How would you feel if you were on the receiving end?

In the next chapter, we'll cover how to handle being broken up with. But for now, take a few minutes to meditate on what it looks like to use the Golden Rule in all your relationships.

CHAPTER 5: HOW TO HANDLE A BREAKUP

"When you're dreaming with a broken heart,
the waking up is the hardest part.
You roll outta bed and down on your knees,
and for a moment you can hardly breathe"
(John Mayer, Dreaming With A Broken Heart).

"But since you've been gone, I can breathe for the first
time. I'm so movin' on. Yeah, yeah"
(Kelly Clarkson, Since U Been Gone)!

B reakups usually happen one of three ways. Maybe your relationship feels more like the first, an epic failure, the second feels more like a relief—or maybe it was mutual.

My friend, Jenn, answered the breakup survey saying,

"Surprisingly the mutual breakup was the hardest on me."

I wonder if you're the one drowning your sorrows in a pint of ice cream.

Or maybe, you're the one who's overjoyed to delete your ex from Facebook, e-mail, and your phone and move on with your life. Either way, I want to share my story, and why I struggled so much with handling breakups.

Although I couldn't help it at times, as long as I can remember I've had anxiety, which is why I overeat. My parents took me to doctor after doctor and they all agreed—I had hypoglycemia. The solution was to carry around extra snacks or protein with me to stabilize my blood sugar when it dipped. The problem was it dipped often.

No matter how much food I ate, I was always hungry. Day after day, I prayed to God and asked Him to stop my hunger.

When eating higher amounts of food didn't work, I became even more anxious. I was afraid to eat because I didn't want to get fat. Even as a young girl, I knew if I became fat, no boy would ever love me.

When my anxiety became so bad that I was afraid to leave the house, my parents took me to the doctor again. Only this time they prescribed Xanax—a little, white, happy pill that made me feel nothing for a few hours, and left me feeling even hungrier after.

I hated that pill!

Taking Xanax made me want to commit suicide. Thankfully, my mom forced me to stop taking it almost immediately. Even after I screamed, cursed, and begged her to continue to let me take medication, I knew it wouldn't fix the problem, but I didn't know where else to turn.

That is, until I learned how to pray (sounds cliché, but it's the truth). The one thing I knew as a preteen was that the only prescription to my anxiety was found in God.

Thank God my mom wasn't afraid to get on her knees and pray with me. She prayed. I prayed. We even asked my pastors to pray over me. With their support, I found the strength to start rebuking each lie the enemy would tell me.

"You're too fat."
"You're too afraid to go outside."
"No boy will ever love you."
"Hunger is bad."

One year later the lies stopped. I'd love to say they stayed away, but they didn't. When they returned, I at least had God by my side, along with my family, and prayer. When the lies became too much to bear, I discovered the power of reading the Bible daily.

That's when I started journaling. That's when I started asking God to heal me daily from anxiety and from my desire to stuff my face full of food.

God has never removed anxiety from my life nor the desire to overeat, but He has brought me through some incredibly tough crisis situations, including a painful breakup over eight years ago.

It took the courage of a nurse to help me see that I was okay. That being hungry was actually normal—and so was anxiety.

I say all of this to encourage you. I'm pretty sure I'm not the only one who struggles with food, overeating, and staying the right weight—and especially breakups.

FORGIVE AND LET GO

It's amazing how much you can learn from a breakup. If you're willing to grow from past relationships, you can be much better for the next person who comes along.

To let a relationship or ex-relationship fully heal, there must be real forgiveness. Not the kind that thinks, wishes, or says nice things to the other person while secretly (or not so secretly) doing the other. It can be even difficult if you struggle with anxiety or overeating like me.

After Marc and I got married, I realized I was carrying around extra pounds from past hurts and a broken relationship. I mention in my book *Forgiving Others, Forgiving Me* that forgiveness affects more than just the physical. Unforgiveness can affect the mind, body, soul, and heart.

I gained more than one hundred pounds because of my bad breakup with Jake. Obviously, it didn't help that I had severe eczema at the time and was taking Prednisone (a total weight gainer). I believe it got much worse because of my unstable emotions.

My inability to stop crying and let go of our failing relationship. When you are in the midst of a breakup, you need passionate patience.

What do I mean by that?

God can handle your passionate, sobbing fits. He can handle your words—even when you feel like cussing. Stop pretending everything is okay. I sure did. I had no idea my body would react so violently. Even when I tried dating again, as I shared in Chapter 2, I just wasn't ready.

In all your worries and "what ifs" concerning any future relationships, can you confidently say God has been faithful? Even in a breakup?

God is not one to change His mind or misdirect your paths. He keeps your feet from slipping—not once, not twice, but many, many times. Timothy, a young apostle for Christ with many health issues, said,

> *"If we endure, we will also reign with him. If we disown him, he will also disown us; if we are faithless, he remains faithful, for he cannot disown himself" (2 Timothy 2:12–14, NIV).*

The same can be said of your life, even when God doesn't feel like enough in the moment. Instead of confronting those who have hurt us as a way of getting even or taking revenge, practice what the Bible says in 1 Thessalonians 5:15.

> *"Make sure that nobody pays back wrong for wrong, but always strive to do what is good for each other and for everybody else."*

DEAL WITH IT

Forgiveness is a process. If there is one phrase that I dislike with a passion, it's "deal with it." Maybe if I was a man I might be more inclined to accept it (not to say that all men aren't emotional).

As a woman I like to let my emotions go wild. What I'm feeling and thinking doesn't always make sense. I'll sometimes camp out in my room and cry or invite a friend over for coffee, so I can talk and make sense of it all. Once I cry or talk it out, or both, I usually feel better. That's my way of dealing with it—whatever is bugging me from my past.

In the midst of a breakup, we can't just deal or give up. There was a time right before I got married when I cried myself to sleep. For an outsider looking in, it wouldn't make much sense.

You'd think I'd be happy, right?

But with a flare-up of eczema, I felt like God rejected me again at my biggest moment of joy. Marriage is the last place I thought I would experience an identity crisis of sorts.

I thought once I got over my last breakup that everything about my future relationship would be okay.

Wrong.

When God brought my husband into my life, I literally had to change my mindset from there are *no* such things as happy endings to God really *does* have plans for a future and a hope. In theory, I was glad to replace it, but my body simply needed more time. I'm going to let you in on a not-so-little secret.

Adjusting from a breakup is never easy, whether it's been eight days, eight months, or eight years (like me).

Psalm 30:5 says, "For his anger lasts only a moment, but his favor lasts a lifetime. Weeping may stay for the night, but rejoicing comes in the morning."

No matter how many times I thought I had overcome my struggle with eczema, anxiety, or overeating, I hadn't.

Maybe you feel the same. Scared. Rejected. Your soul feels trapped. Caged. It can be hard to continue on after a painful breakup. Thankfully, we serve a God who is the source of all comfort. In Isaiah 40:1–2, it says,

"Comfort, comfort my people says your God. Speak tenderly to [insert your name here], and proclaim to her that her hard service has been completed, that her sin has been paid for, that she has received from the Lord's hand double for all her sins" (NIV).

And Isaiah 41:9b–10 says, "You are my servant; I have chosen you and have not rejected you. So do not fear, for I am with you; do not be dismayed, for I am your God. I will strengthen you and help you; I will uphold you with my righteous right hand" (NIV).

WHAT A RELIEF!

At this point, I can see a few of you rolling your eyes. You may be saying,

"So what? I'm sorry for your bad breakup, but mine wasn't like that."

Maybe you've never been through a painful breakup (or no breakup at all). Newsflash: not every relationship ends badly.

The second way people handle a breakup is the conscious choice to move on in faith. In other words, you are relieved. The only piece of advice or encouragement is the power of prayer.

Whether you can barely breathe or you're breathing for the first time, it's important to stay mindful in prayer, because eventually our strength runs out.

Colossians 4:2 says, "Devote yourselves to prayer, being watchful and thankful" (NIV).

A relationship should encourage our daily habits of readings of the Bible and devotionals. Don't let bitterness creep back in. Hurt, fear, and sadness may develop over time if we let it. That's when gratitude waits for us.

"Gratitude unleashes the freedom to live content in the moment, rather than being anxious about the future or regretting the past."[8]

Choose gratitude over your breakup. Like putting on clothes in the morning, you shouldn't date naked. Learn to cultivate a thankful heart. Seek joy. Happiness is just a feeling, but gratitude is a lifestyle.

IT'S MUTUAL

If your breakup was mutual, rejoice! A mutual decision between two people is the third and final way people handle a breakup.

I've had a few of these, but I wouldn't consider myself technically dating. It's hard to keep emotions in check when a relationship has lasted long enough for one or both people to become attached. The verse that comes to mind is from Psalm 18:19–20, which says,

"He brought me out into a spacious place; he rescued me because he delighted in me. The Lord has dealt with me according to my righteousness; according to the cleanness of my hands he has rewarded me" (NIV).

David called this his place of safety or spacious place. He also respected God's boundaries (Psalm 16:6). David was in his room with a view when he noticed Bathsheba.

"In the spring, at the time when kings normally go out to war…David remained in Jerusalem" (2 Samuel 11:1, NIV).

David had stopped fighting. I'm not sure if he was hurt or if he was genuinely tired of fighting. He was up on the rooftop of his palace enjoying his view. That's when he noticed Bathsheba's naked body.

Yowza.

What happens next is a tragedy. All because of his palace view. He couldn't just watch her bathe. He had to have her.

I find it's easier to slip quietly into sin when we're comfortable. A contented heart, believe it or not, is something to take very seriously because it's when we least expect to sin.

In the midst of a breakup, God provides our very own safe place. Like David, he honors our fierce fighting. Our innocence. But it's when we stop that we need to careful. After David had sinned, he acknowledged God and said,

"Against you, only you, have I sinned and done what is evil in your sight" (Psalm 51:4, NIV).

Maybe you haven't struggled at all. Maybe you've undergone a horrendous breakup. Maybe others of you have struggled on the battlefield of lust or pornography and you're not sure how to ask God to forgive you.

I'm so glad David's example is in the Bible. God forgave his indiscretions just as He forgives our sin today. We can thank God for that! If you would like to learn how to live in the freedom, to remain in the room with a view and stay there, continue on to the next chapter.

PART III: RELEARNING SINGLEHOOD

CHAPTER 6: BE YOUR OWN PERSON

"It takes courage to grow up and become who you really are" (e. e. cummings).

I remember sitting cross-legged under my parent's coffee table. I was busy writing while my boyfriend at the time, Jake, was also in the living room. We were making plans to see each other again. He lived on the East Coast and I on the West Coast, and since we didn't have much money, we knew it would be a while until the next flight.

Back then I had the kind of blind faith that could move mountains. I didn't look at the circumstances but at God's promises. Since I thought Jake was the one for me, his attention gave me the inspiration and the confidence I needed to write out my first book. I was nineteen then. It wasn't long until I finished, cross-legged and all, writing my first manuscript. Each chapter started with a Bible verse and a promise from God.

I don't know which was longer, my manuscript or the time we dated. In a quick burst of writing passion, I was done with the book and my relationship was over again, but this time I knew it was permanent. I knew better than to cry anymore tears over this boy. I knew that God was in the healing business, because my skin had healed since my first breakup with Jake. Six years it took for me to realize God had a better story for me; otherwise, why else would He let me suffer, right?

Instead of letting my bitterness (because I let Jake in one last time) get me down, my confusion led me deep into the heart of Texas.

I decided it was time for me to be my own person.

I moved to Texas and joined a nine-month-long Discipleship Training School called Ambassadors For Christ and said goodbye to my friends and family. I couldn't wait to learn more about writing and the Word. I had so many more questions than answers. I thought I had heard God right about Jake. I thought that He said he was "the one" for me.

I was wrong again.

How could I be so stupid?

I hadn't yet learned it's actually possible to hear what you only want to hear. It's easy to mistake God's voice for my own because all I could hear was the sound of my heartbreak. I understood God's comfort, but I had yet to understand His ways.

I found God in Texas. Ambassadors For Christ provided an excellent outlet for me to meet like-minded people and join the Jerry B. Jenkins Christian Writer's Guild. I didn't know it yet, but that would be the tool God used to shape me as a writer and teach me everything I needed to know.

I sure wasn't ready for my first lesson: you have to let your dreams die before they can fully succeed.

After living in Texas a few months, my eczema came back and I had to move home. I felt like a failure. I felt if I couldn't serve God, then what else could I possibly do?

I was done. Finished. Not only was I confused about my identity (who I was) but my place in His kingdom. I knew I had a unique personality. I was the loudest introvert you'll ever meet. I had seen God heal me once, and now I could only hope He'd do it again.

Three years later, God healed me.

That's a total of ten years I waited on God to fulfill my dreams of becoming a writer. During those ten years, I wrote and wrote and wrote, but did nothing with it. I didn't think it was any good. It was my own private journal writings between God and me. Talk about angry conversations, wet tears, and desperate pleas.

When God finally healed me, I wanted to forget about writing. I wanted to live my life and be my own person. I didn't want a boyfriend to define me. I also didn't want to be reminded of my past. Since my journals were a painful reminder of my past, I needed time to live and process and create a whole new story.

I was used to creating a new story. I had done it once, twice, and now I was going to do it for the third time.

This time I was ready. I got a job that didn't mean anything to me emotionally. I couldn't handle one more emotion. I learned what business looked like. I finished my college degree. I did things for me because I knew someday I'd need them. I also bought my own car and established good credit. I moved out of my parent's house again. I lived with roommates I didn't get along with and roommates that I did.

It wasn't until I turned twenty-six that I felt a deep longing that couldn't be filled. I told God I thought it was time for me to get married because I was tired of being my own person.

I ached for a partner. I wanted to be married in the worst way. I had had enough of this figuring myself out. I was sick and tired of being my own person. It's funny looking back because there were moments of true contentment and moments of feeling like God abandoned my desires—or worse—forgot them completely.

I'm sure I'm not the only person who wished to share my life with someone, but instead of hearing God's voice of comfort, you get silence.

LOST AND FOUND

It's in the death of a vision and the death of a dream that I found myself again. I fought hard for a job that I cared about. I started writing again. I picked up my old manuscripts and wrote new ones. I acquired an agent and kept up my blog. That's when I got my first book contract, and then another, and another, and another.

I found grace.

I found myself in the very same pages where I rejected myself for who I was.

I let go of past hurts, future fears, and learned to live in the present. My desire for a mate never went away, but I didn't let it control me as much. I moved out of my parent's house for what seemed like the hundredth time. I applied for seminary and assumed I'd be single forever.

That's when I met Marc. Please trust me when I say I *wasn't* content. I am the kind of person who is never satisfied with my relationship with God. I just hate that stupid cliché that so many married and/or older adults tell young people.

"It's not until you're satisfied in God that He'll bring you someone."

I was far from content. If nothing else, it was the complete opposite. I told God that He was *late*, and I tried to do my own thing because I was tired of all the waiting around.

I'm sure God chuckled about my attitude, but that didn't stop Him from bringing me "the one." Some days I look back on my past and think,

"If only I knew."

If only my former self knew God could and would bring my future husband to me in spite of my attitude. He certainly didn't need my help. It wasn't up to me to be the perfect Christian and try to help Him along.

Wrong.

Recently, I wrote a letter to my former self because there are a few things that I know now that I didn't know then, but wished I did. It is my hope that after reading this letter you might try in your own words to write a letter as well. Who knows, maybe you'll realize you really are being your own person!

LETTER TO MY FORMER SELF

I wish I could invent a time machine so I could go back and tell you a secret. Also, tell you how beautiful and brave and fierce you have become. A woman who loves God and isn't afraid to show it.

Many girls wish they had your confidence.

You may not believe that now, but someday you'll see it.

Then I'd tell my former self the secret I've been dying to tell her: you WILL meet your handsome prince.

You will not be single forever. You will lose weight and find another, better job.

I know she's held on to that prayer request for years—cherished it in her heart even. Hoped. Prayed for that day when she'd no longer be single.

I wish I could tell her not to grow bitter and jaded because of her *single* relationship status.

It makes me so sad to look back at my former self and see her lose all hope. She thought she had nothing left to give. That her world was over. It wasn't, although it was sure close.

I wish I could tell her that her dreams of working in ministry alongside her husband will come true, just not the way she expected but better. That's the part she gave up on. I so, so wish she stopped assuming things about her future.

I wish she had just let her prayers climb and continue climbing higher and higher until they reached the throne room of God.

Her future husband wasn't to be found through online dating, but she already knew that.

Her future husband was busy like her and needed more time. (This was a good thing.) She just needed to find herself first. (This was and still is the most important thing.)

No relationship can compare to the God-sized-shaped hole in her heart. No matter how incredible or handsome her future husband would be, I wish my former self knew what it meant to rely on God fully for everything. Even when she felt she had accomplished this many times, there would be no amount of times that would ever be enough.

Why?

Because God is a jealous God.

It's okay to spend time with Him. It's okay to even think of it as wasted time because God never thinks that.

It's okay to vent to God. He can take it. It's okay to have panic attacks, feel like losing control, and loathe living back in Mom and Dad's house. God can take that, too. He can take all of it, and He still loves her.

Most of all I wish I could travel back in time to give my former self a hug. Then I'd muster up all the grace in the world and tell her to learn true humility. My former self always had a tendency to think she knew it all. That she was in control, and knew the perfect timing for everything.

There are times I wish I could have slapped her in the face while other times I would have punched her. No matter what, I knew she wouldn't listen.

But she did listen when God broke her. Over and over, He broke her. It still breaks my heart to this day knowing how tough she tried to be.

How long she tried to hold it all together for the sake of what others thought. Thankfully, God did answer her prayers. He brought an amazing man into her life. He kept the secret that I wanted so desperately to share with my former self four years ago.

ASK GOD

If you are still waiting on your future husband or wife, ask God. Then keep asking Him. He can handle it. I know it can be hard to persevere through the silence. Please don't interpret God's lack of a response on His lack of care.

Psalm 30:5 says, "For his anger lasts only a moment, but his favor lasts a lifetime; weeping may remain for a night, but rejoicing comes in the morning" (NIV).

Maybe your crying will last thirty more mornings. Maybe it's three hundred more.

Will you promise me one thing though?

Don't give up hope. I know it's a promise I shared with you earlier that I struggled with, but it's one I wish I would have kept and I hope you'll at least consider.

"Against all hope, Abraham in hope believed and so became the father of many nations, just as it had been said to him, 'So shall your offspring be.' Without weakening in his faith, he faced the fact that his body was as good as dead—since he was about a hundred years old—and that Sarah's womb was also dead. Yet he did not waver through unbelief regarding the promise of God, but was strengthened in his faith and gave glory to God, being fully persuaded that God had power to do what he had promised" (Romans 4:18–21, NIV).

In the last chapter, we'll learn where love comes from, and how it can change your life!

CHAPTER 7: HE LOVES ME!

"This is how God showed his love among us: He sent his one and only Son into the world that we might live through him. We love because he first loved us" (1 John 4:9, 19).

I f you've made it this far, *congratulations*! The fact is you are loved. End of story. Happily ever after. Period. There's a reason why so many people talk about fairy tales and romance, because God designed our lives to fit into the size of His love, which cannot be measured. Because God's love is so big, it's hard to grasp this concept. But this is my prayer:

"That out of his glorious riches he may strengthen you with power through his Spirit in your inner being, so that Christ may dwell in your hearts through faith. And I pray that you, being rooted and established in love, may have the power, together with all the saints, to grasp how wide and long and high and deep is the love of Christ" (Ephesians 3:16–18, NIV).

NO MORE HEARTBREAK

Maybe you're not so sure. You're not buying what I'm selling. You're not sold on the idea of a God who loves you—personally and unconditionally.

Did you know the word "bride" is found at least forty times in the Bible?

That's not to mention the words "wife," "husband," or "beloved." If you call yourself a Christian, God considers you His beloved.

"I will betroth you to me forever; I will betroth you in righteousness and justice, in love and compassion. I will betroth you in faithfulness, and you will acknowledge the Lord" (Hosea 2:19–20, NIV).

Breakups sting because our hearts were never meant to experience heartbreak. The tree Adam and Eve ate from is called The Tree of the Knowledge of Good and Evil (Genesis 3:5). It's interesting that it wasn't enough for them to know; they had to taste and experience this (good versus evil). I got this idea from Ray Bentley, my pastor, who shared recently just how crafty the enemy was.

He chose his words carefully while deceiving Adam and Eve (who took the first bite). They already knew God. It was through this close and personal fellowship with God that they talked about all things.

Even evil.

But it wasn't enough for Adam and Eve to talk about the meaning of evil with God. They had to experience it for themselves. That's when sin entered the world. It didn't take long for heartbreak (sin) to take effect.

Soon Adam and Eve experienced loss. Cain, their first-born son, murdered their second-born son, Abel.

Can you imagine the guilt they must have felt for disobeying God, yet also the experience of grace when Eve gave birth to Seth, their third child (Genesis 4:25)?

As you navigate the realm of relationships in your own life, I encourage you to ask God to give you the wisdom to choose each relationship wisely.

Proverbs 12:26 (NIV) says, "The righteous choose their friends carefully, but the way of the wicked leads them astray."

The hard part is letting God determine who is good. That means no rebounds. No one-night stands. No more hiding.

Pursuing relationships peacefully and cautiously is a mandate designed by God for our protection. Proverbs 12:26 doesn't say you should only be careful with opposite sex friendships—it's *both*. Boundaries should be important with same-sex friendships too.

All this time, I was taught growing up in the church that I was supposed to guard my heart against men. What I didn't realize was how reckless I was with my female friends.

I feel like it took me getting married to open my eyes to heartbreak—not just with the opposite sex. I feel like my marriage cost me my best friend. It was the same girlfriend who promised to be there for me through heartache (and she was), but as soon as life flipped and it was her turn to be there for me in my joy, she couldn't. It was so painful to lose a best friend because I gained a husband.

The ultimate test of friendship—male or female—is time, which is why I believe it's important to be careful. Instead of jumping from one relationship into another, choose your friends wisely—even the ones who help you overcome heartbreak.

PENNY FOR YOUR THOUGHTS

Below is a random sampling from the last part of the survey I want to share. It doesn't surprise me how many people mentioned God and friends as allies after heartbreak. The best memories I had as a single person were all those hangout times with my best girl friends. It is cool to see how many times God brought a new friend into my life at just the right time.

When I was getting over Jake, God brought Jenn and Amy into my life. When I was having a hard time after moving back from Texas, He brought Rachel, Summer, Bryan, Monique, and many others.

I wonder who that is in your life?

Maybe write them a quick text and tell them how much you appreciate him or her today! Here are a few quotes—or should I say pennies—that I gathered of some of your thoughts of getting over a breakup:

Jennifer, 31, said: "Knowing that I had God as my comforter as well as my dear friends that were always there. It was knowing that God had something better for my future."

Tara, 30, said: "Well, moving 3,000 miles away definitely helped healing in the long run. But I have to say initially faith in Jesus, counseling, good friends, and watching *Tyler Perry's Diary of a Mad Black Woman* over and over again. Seriously!"

Mandy, 36, said: "Faith, friends."

Caroline, 28, said: "A good friend during and after a breakup is priceless. I had both women and platonic male friends who were pillars of support. I could cry to them, ask them questions that had no answers, and even hypothesize with them for weeks afterward. If they were sick of it, it never showed. Their loyalty to me and their unwavering belief that there was better out there waiting for me, just beyond the horizon, really helped me survive those first few weeks."

Shannon, 27, said: "The Lord, friends, and family. Lots of worship music."

Andrea, 24, said: "Reading and yoga."

Stacey, 34, said: "My in-laws helped me a ton. Couldn't have made it through the divorce without God either."

Stephanie, 26, said: "My family/friends who were there for me helped immensely. When I broke up and knew I was following God's plan, it was helpful. But when I was broken up with and didn't have a clue, there wasn't much that could make me feel better except for hope that God's plan was best."

Nicole, 24, said: "At the time I wasn't a Christian, so I depended on myself. It was really hard, but it forced me to change my life in dramatic ways and start focusing on me. I started going to the gym and eating healthy. I also stopped hanging out with the group of friends I was hanging out with, because they were headed in a bad direction. I became very independent and strong, but at the same time very closed (I built walls to protect myself)."

Amber, 23, said: "There were times in my relationship with my husband before we got married that the thought of breaking up may have crossed my mind. Even now in my marriage, I've had the thought of if we had broken up for a while in the six years of dating before getting married. During those times, being able to run and tell on him to God, journal my prayers, and get counseling from a godly mentor helped me."

Monique, 36, said: "God, family, friends. As hard as it was to get out of the house, making sure I did not isolate myself was key."

Katie, 22, said: "My parents helped me a lot emotionally, because I was always conveniently on my way home or at home when the breakups occurred. And my best friend has always been there for me to help me de-boy my room and get my mind off of the breakup."

Michael, 27, said: "It was not funny, but godly counsels and Bible reading helped a lot."

Brenda, 22, said: "My family, Christian mentor, and best friends."

Jennifer, 33, said: "God and my friends were good support."

Alicia, 29, said: "Taylor Swift and Kelly Clarkson."

D.D., 28, said: "Confidence in God's leading through trustworthy counsel, Bible reading, prayer, busyness, summer sunshine, and remembering to be grateful."

Alexandrea, 27, said: "Definitely crying and just allowing myself to feel sad rather than trying to pretend like I'm not feeling what I'm feeling. After awhile, I do try to get busy and maybe visit family or hang out with my friends. I also spend a lot of time watching movies (which is something I love to do as a hobby of mine). I wrote in my journal a lot during that time, and I talked with someone. If the breakup is very difficult, I will definitely go to counseling and have done so multiple times."

YOU ARE LOVED

After reading through this list and this book, I hope you remember one thing:

You.
Are.
Loved.

God loved you first, so you could love others. He never meant for you to experience heartbreak, and He is the only one who can heal us physically, emotionally, and spiritually.

So what if you meet your dream guy or girl soon?

God wants us to love and obey Him because we want to, not because we have to. If you've seen the movie The Break-Up with Vince Vaughn and Jennifer Aniston, that was the point. Jennifer's character broke up with Vince because he didn't act like he wanted to be with her. All she wanted was for him to at least try to act like he cared about their relationship.

Maybe your heart says one thing but your actions do another.

Did you know your actions speak your heart?

If your heart is not fully with God, the lover of your soul, then something's missing.

God desperately wants you all to Himself. Keep your faith in God and that He will bring you the desires of your heart. Stand strong and do not look to the opposite sex. Do not be hindered by your flesh, for your flesh wants pleasure now. But now is not the time. Not yet.

Do not be frustrated; the day is coming. Do not be angry. When the day comes, you will be pleased beyond comprehension. Wait for your future spouse and do not anxiously search for him or her. When the time is ripe, you will know because God will show you.

When you give this to God, He will give you peace, and when attacks of the flesh come, flee for the peace God has, which comes when you trust in Him and wait for the right timing. The time, when it comes, will be amazing, so please wait for this wonderful gift.

Jesus loves you.

NOTES

1. Originally Appeared in: RelevantMagazine.com, "Why Guarding Your Heart Isn't Enough," March 7, 2012. http://www.relevantmagazine.com/life/relationship/features/28518-why-guarding-your-heart-isnt-enough.

2. Timothy Keller with Kathy Keller, *The Meaning of Marriage*, (New York, NY: Dutton, 2011), 115.

3. John & Stasi Eldredge, *Captivating*, (Nashville, TN: Thomas Nelson, 2005), 58.

4. "Heartbreak." *Merriam-Webster Online Dictionary*. Merriam-Webster, Inc. http://www.merriam-webster.com/dictionary/heartbreak.

5. Lettie B. Cowma and Jim Reimannn, *Streams in the Desert*, (Grand Rapids, MI: Zondervan, 2008), 69.

6. John & Stasi Eldredge, *Captivating*, (Nashville, TN: Thomas Nelson, 2005), 143.

7. Charles Ringma, *Seize the Day with Dietrich Bonhoeffer*, (Colorado Springs, CO: NavPress, 2000), March 17.

8. Ellen Vaughn, *Radical Gratitude*, (Grand Rapids, MI: Zondervan, 2005), 203.

ABOUT THE AUTHOR

enee Fisher is a spirited speaker, coach, consultant and author, who published her first eight books in under eight years. A self-proclaimed "Dream Defender," Renee is passionate about calling dreams to life in others. A graduate of Biola University, she lives in Austin, Texas with her handsome husband and their fur child named "Star." Connect at ReneeFisher.com.

PREVIOUS WORKS:

Faithbook of God
Dream Devotional
Forgiving Others, Forgiving Me
Not Another Dating Book
Faithbook of Jesus

OTHER BOOKS INCLUDING RENEE:

It's A New Beginning by Willie Alfonso
NIV Bible for Women

CPSIA information can be obtained
at www.ICGtesting.com
Printed in the USA
LVOW10s1344010318
568334LV00019B/649/P